FILM PHOTOGRAPHY
POCKET GUIDE

TABLE OF CONTENTS

PRE-SHOOT CHECKLIST

01 WORKING WITH 35MM FILM

A NOTE ABOUT 35MM FILM CAMERAS 5
TYPES OF 35MM FILM 6
35MM FILM AND ISO 8
LOADING 35MM FILM 9
AFTER SHOOTING: WINDING YOUR FILM 12
GETTING YOUR FILM DEVELOPED AND SCANNED 13

02 EXPOSURE BASICS

APERTURE AND DEPTH OF FIELD 15
SHUTTER SPEED AND MOTION 16
ISO, GRAIN, AND WHITE BALANCE 17
STOPS 17

03 SHOOTING IN MANUAL MODE

USING YOUR CAMERA'S LIGHT METER 19
THE "SUNNY 16" RULE 20
EXPOSURE CHART FOR SHOOTING FILM 21

04 BEYOND MANUAL MODE

EXPOSURE/SHOOTING MODES 22
METERING MODES 23
EXPOSURE COMPENSATION 24
FOCUS AREA AND FOCUS MODES 25
RELEASE/DRIVE MODES 26

05 LENSES AND FOCAL LENGTH

FOCAL LENGTHS 27
LENS COMPRESSION AND DISTORTION 29
FOCAL LENGTH, CAMERA SHAKE, AND SHUTTER SPEED 31
IMAGE STABILIZATION/VIBRATION REDUCTION 31

06 ADVANCED SHOOTING TECHNIQUES

BACK BUTTON FOCUS 32
FOCUS AND COMPOSITION 32
BRACKETING EXPOSURES 33
PUSHING AND PULLING FILM 34

07 COMPOSITION TIPS AND SHOOTING SCENARIOS

RULE OF THIRDS 36
FILL THE FRAME 37
NEGATIVE SPACE 38
LEADING LINES 39
PATTERNS AND REPETITION 40
FRAME WITHIN A FRAME 41

POINT OF VIEW 42
COLOR 43
BLACK AND WHITE 44
WATCH THE BACKGROUND 45
SIMPLIFY 46
FIND GREAT LIGHT 47
PORTRAIT 48
GROUP PORTRAIT 49
LANDSCAPE 50
FREEZE ACTION 51
SHOWING MOTION—PANNING 52
LOW-LIGHT SITUATIONS 53
LONG EXPOSURE 54
MACRO/CLOSE-UP 55

PRE-SHOOT CHECKLIST

Check these settings before you head out with your camera!

SETTING	MY PREFERRED SETTING
☑ Film Loaded in Camera	....
☑ ISO Dial Setting on Camera Matches ISO of Film: Yes/No	....
☑ Pushing/Pulling Film: Yes/No	....
☑ Additional Film in Camera Bag	....
☑ Light Meter (or Light Meter app)	....

If applicable:

☑ Battery Fully Charged and In Camera	....
☑ Exposure/Shooting Mode	....
☑ Metering Mode	....
☑ Exposure Compensation	....
☑ Focus Area	....
☑ Focus Mode	....
☑ Release/Drive Mode	....
☑ Lens Image Stabilization/ Vibration Reduction: On/Off	....

01 WORKING WITH 35MM FILM

Before we dive into getting great shots with your camera, let's take a moment to discuss 35mm cameras and film.

A NOTE ABOUT 35MM FILM CAMERAS

Even though digital cameras are dominant today, there is still a wide range of available 35mm film cameras that you can use, from manual-only cameras to advanced film cameras that have nearly all the same features as today's digital cameras.

In this Pocket Guide, the way we'll approach such a range of possibilities is to assume you have a manual-only camera when it comes to loading and unloading film. As for shooting, we have a dedicated section called "Shooting in Manual Mode" if you are a manual-only shooter. And in "Beyond Manual Mode," we'll discuss a number of features that more advanced film cameras could have, which you also might want to use.

TYPES OF 35MM FILM

There are a lot of great film stocks on the market today. A few popular ones are listed below to get you started. The best way to find a film look that you like is to try out a bunch of different film stocks and see what works best for you.

There are three types of film available: black-and-white, color negative, and slide film.

Black-and-white film: This film is by far the easiest to use, as it comes in a variety of ISO speeds and can even be developed at home. Examples of popular black-and-white film stocks include Ilford HP5 Plus 400, Kodak Tri-X 400, and Ilford Delta 3200.

Color negative film: When using this film stock (also called C-41), the brightest parts of the image appear darkest on the film negative, and the darkest areas appear lightest. The color negative is then reversed when scanning or printing. Color negative film offers the widest range of ISO speeds and has much better exposure latitude, especially compared to color slide film. This means that your exposures can be a little off and still produce great images. So if you're just starting out, give black-and-white and color negative film a try first.

A few popular color negative film stocks are Kodak Portra 400, Fujifilm Superia X-Tra 400, Kodak Gold 200, and Fujifilm Fujicolor 200. The Fuji brand is known for its greens and blues, while Kodak is known for yellows and reds. Kodak Portra is especially loved for its rendition of skin tones.

Slide film: This film stock (also called E-6) produces a positive image on a transparent film—the image does not need to be reversed like in color negative film. This means you can just hold it up to the light (or put it in a slide projector) and see the image. Slide film has a very narrow exposure latitude, meaning you really have to nail the exposure when you take the photo. The advantages of slide film are tight grain, lower ISO, and vivid colors. The slides will also last longer as slim negatives can degrade more rapidly than slides.

Examples of slide/color reversal film are Kodak Ektachrome 100 and Fujifilm Velvia 50.

In addition to those listed above, check out Cinestill and Lomography film stocks.

Note: If you're storing your film for a while, keep it in a Ziploc bag in the fridge. This will help preserve it. Before shooting, let it come to room temperature.

35MM FILM AND ISO

What do numbers like 100, 200, 400, 800, 1600, and 3200 at the end of the film name mean? Those numbers are the ISO speed rating, which lets you know how sensitive the film is to light. ISO 100 is less sensitive to light, so it's made for situations with lots of light (such as bright, sunny days), and ISO 800 and higher is for low-light situations (indoors, for example), or situations where you need a very fast shutter speed (such as when shooting action).

Lots of photographers agree that ISO 400 is a nice middle ground for most of the various situations you'll encounter when shooting film.

If you are familiar with shooting digitally, you likely know that one of the advantages of digital photography is that you can change the ISO whenever you want, which makes your camera's digital sensor more or less sensitive to light. This is helpful when you're shooting in different lighting conditions. But when shooting film, you are committed to using that roll of film until you've taken all the available exposures, and you can't change the ISO from shot to shot.

LOADING 35MM FILM

Here are the main steps for loading a roll of 35mm into your camera:

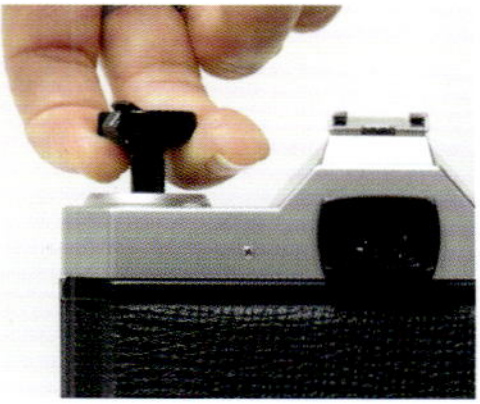

1. Open the camera back. (Make sure there's not unexposed film in your camera!) On most manual-only cameras, you do this by pulling up the rewind spool.

2. Insert the film canister into the rewind spool's slot, then push the rewind spool all the way back down. Also be sure to know the ISO of the film you're loading (you'll need that in step 6).

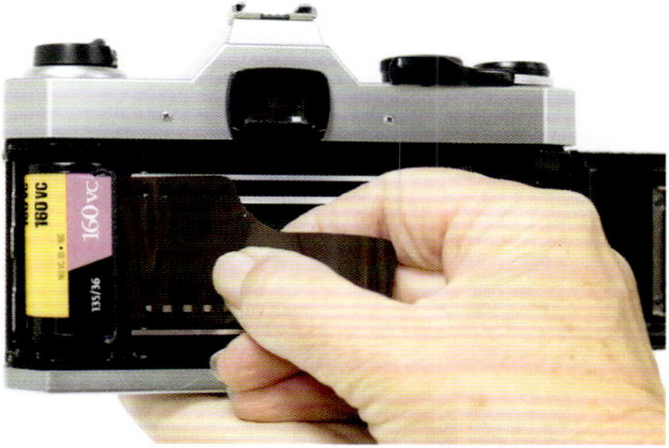

3. Take the "leader" of the film (the part of film sticking out from the film canister) and feed it into the take-up spool on the other side, lining up the sprockets with the film's sprocket openings. Wind your film just a bit to make it taut.

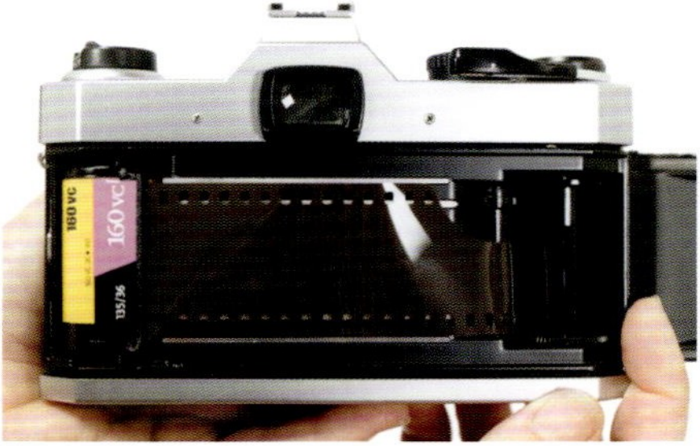

4. Close the camera back tightly.

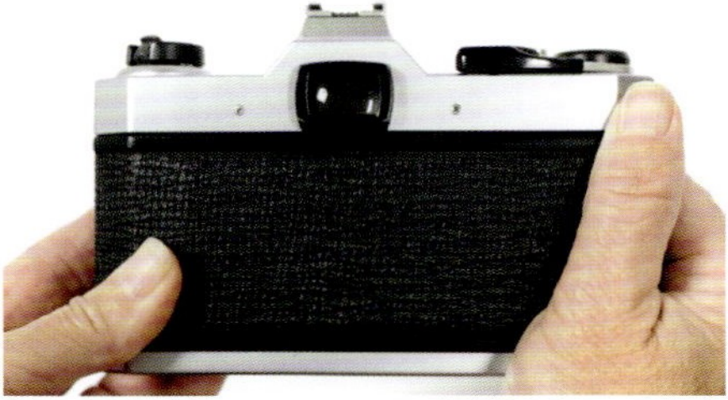

5. Wind the film (A) and—this is important!—watch the rewind spool (B) on the other side of the camera to make sure it is also turning. This confirms that the film is winding from the roll and didn't come loose from the take-up spool.

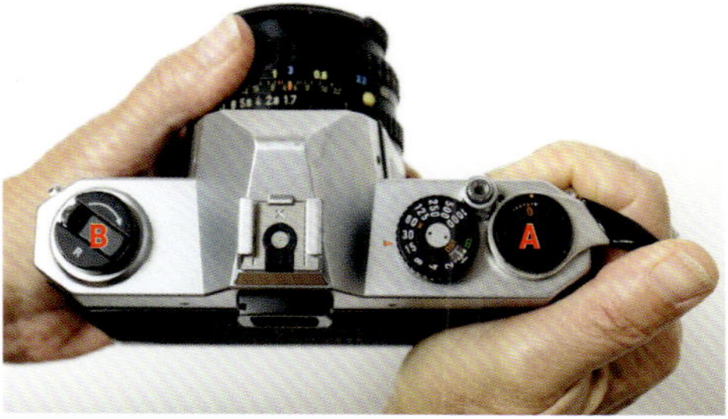

6. With the camera back closed, fire off two images to advance the film to get to a part that hasn't yet been exposed to light, and now you're ready to shoot. On most cameras, the counter dial should now show 0, and will advance every time you take a shot. Also, be sure to set the ISO dial on the camera to the ISO of the film you're shooting.

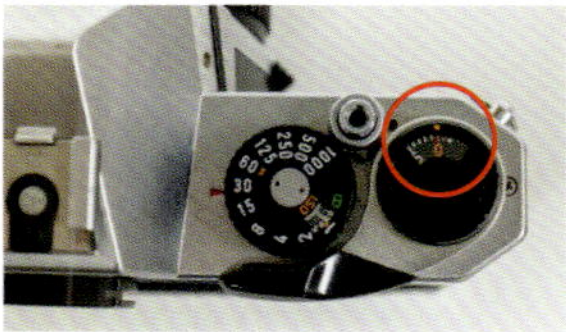

AFTER SHOOTING: WINDING YOUR FILM

Once you've shot the entire roll of film, it's time to rewind your film and send it off to a film developing lab.

To rewind your film: Use the rewind knob on the rewind spool to wind your film back into its original canister. Note: On many cameras, there is a rewind button or lock you need to push to enable you to activate the rewind spool.

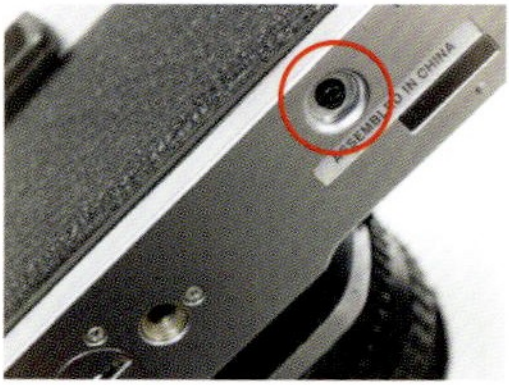

The rewind button on the bottom of a Pentax K1000

Make sure all the film is wound back into the canister before opening the camera back so that you don't expose any film to light. You will usually feel a release of tension when the last bit of film comes off the take-up spool and winds into the canister.

GETTING YOUR FILM DEVELOPED AND SCANNED

If you're just getting started with shooting 35mm film, it's completely fine to take your film to a neighborhood photo center (such as Walgreens) for development and scanning. It's exciting to see how the photos turned out!

Once you get the hang of shooting 35mm film, you may want to send your film to a dedicated photo lab where you'll be sure to get the best development, scans, and service. Be sure to check out your local camera store for their options and recommendations.

You can also check out these online photo labs: Richard Photo Lab (richardphotolab.com), The Find Lab (thefindlab.com), The Darkroom (thedarkroom.com), and MPIX (mpix.com).

02 EXPOSURE BASICS

The exposure is the overall amount of light that reaches the film for the creation of a photograph. You want just the right amount of light to create a well-exposed image. Too bright? Your photo is overexposed. Too dark? Your photo is underexposed. These are the three settings that control the exposure:

Aperture: The size of the opening in the lens, which controls how much light enters the lens at once

Shutter speed: Controls the amount of time that the film is exposed to light

ISO: Tells you how sensitive the film is to light

In addition to these settings controlling how much light reaches your film, the aperture and shutter speed also have very important creative effects, which influence the look of the photo.

When creating a photograph, you want to do two things:
1) get the right amount of light onto the film to create a good exposure, and 2) achieve the creative look you want.

APERTURE AND DEPTH OF FIELD

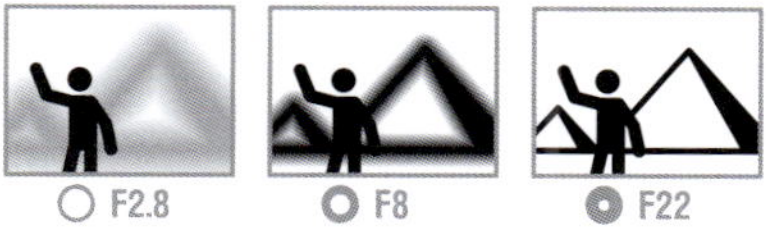

The aperture—which is described in terms of f/stops: f/2.8, f/4, f/5.6, etc.—is the opening in the lens that lets light into the camera and onto your film. It seems counterintuitive, but:

- The smaller the f/number, the larger the opening. For example, f/2.8 is a wide opening that lets a lot of light into the camera.
- The larger the f/number, the smaller the opening. For example, f/22 is a narrow opening that lets very little light into the camera.

Creative effect: The aperture also controls the depth of field in an image, which determines how much of the image is in focus from the foreground to the background. The larger the aperture (such as f/2.8), the shallower the depth of field. Shallow depth of field is often used for portraits. The smaller the aperture (such as f/22), the deeper the depth of field. Deep depth of field is often used in landscape photography.

SHUTTER SPEED AND MOTION

1/500 1/60 1/8

The shutter speed is the amount of time that light reaches the film:

- Faster shutter speeds, such as 1/500" or 1/4000", allow less light to reach the film.
- Longer shutter speeds, such as 1/15" or 1 second, allow more light to reach the film. (Sometimes photographers will use very long shutter speeds of several minutes or even hours.)

Creative effect: Shutter speed controls how motion is shown in the image. The faster the shutter speed, the less time your subject has to move in your scene, and thus the greater the chance that the subject will be frozen in sharp focus. Alternatively, slow shutter speeds can show the motion of the subject as a blurred effect. For example, a fast shutter speed might be used to freeze water droplets, while a slow shutter speed could be used to blur the flowing water of a waterfall, creating a "silky waterfall" look.

ISO, GRAIN, AND WHITE BALANCE

The ISO setting determines how sensitive to light the film is. The higher the ISO setting, the more sensitive the film is. At higher ISO settings, film grain can be noticeably seen in your photos. A lot of film photographers love the look of film grain! Another characteristic of film is its white balance. Some film stock is meant for Daylight, other film for Tungsten (indoor lighting), etc. It's often best to stick with a white balance that matches the lighting conditions you're shooting in, but you can also use this creatively in your photography.

STOPS

In photography, light is measured and referred to in terms of "stops." A one-stop difference in exposure is equivalent to either doubling or halving the amount of light that reaches the film. Aperture and shutter speed can be adjusted in increments of one stop (or even in 1/3-stop increments on some cameras):

- Aperture: f/stop increments of one stop are f/2, f/2.8, f/4, f/5.6, f/8, f/11, f/16, etc.
- Shutter speed: The options for one-stop increments are 1", 1/2", 1/4", 1/8", 1/15", 1/30", 1/60", 1/125", etc.
- ISO: One-stop increments in ISO are 100, 200, 400, 800, 1600, 3200, etc. (This is helpful to know when selecting which film stock to use in different lighting conditions. For example, ISO 800 film is twice as sensitive to light as ISO 400.)

As an example, if a photo is overexposed (too much light), you might "stop down" the exposure by one stop by making either of the following adjustments:

- Aperture: Change from f/2.8 to f/4—letting in half as much light at once.
- Shutter speed: Change from 1/30" to 1/60"—cutting in half the amount of time that light reaches the film.

How will you know if your film photo is overexposed or not? You won't know until the film is developed later! That's why some photographers "bracket" their exposures to be on the safe side. More on that on page 33.

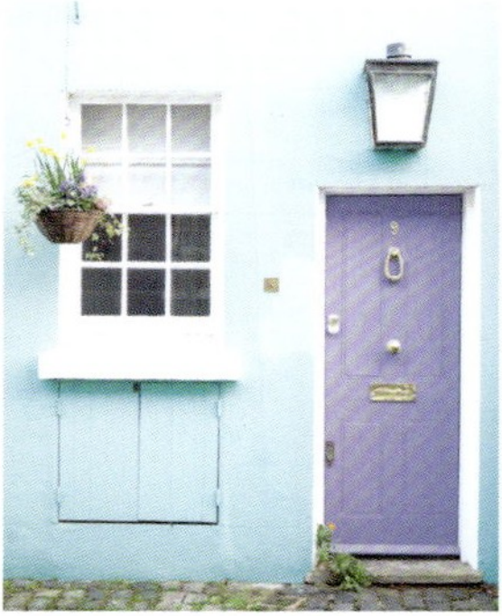

Overexposed by one stop

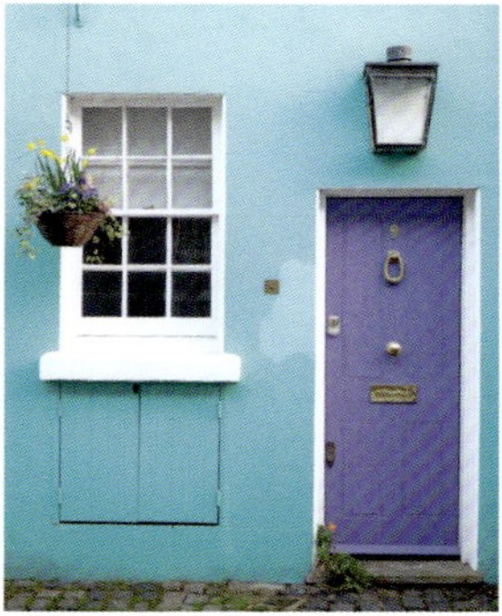

Exposure corrected by changing aperture from f/2.8 to f/4

03 SHOOTING IN MANUAL MODE

USING YOUR CAMERA'S LIGHT METER

When shooting in manual mode, you need to be able to determine the correct aperture and shutter speed settings in order to get the right amount of light onto the film. The way to do this is by using a light meter. Happily, most film cameras have a built-in light meter.

The light meter measures the light coming into the camera lens and helps you determine the right combination of aperture and shutter speed, in combination with your film's ISO, to create a proper exposure. A "proper exposure" is, of course, subjective, but the light meter is trying to give you an exposure where the light in the scene averages out to an overall "middle gray."

Once you set the ISO dial on the camera to match the ISO of your film, then you're ready to use the built-in light meter. If, for example, you're shooting a portrait and know that you want a shallow depth of field, then you can set your aperture to f/2.8, and then adjust the shutter speed until the light meter's needle/indicator lines up in the center of the scale.

As noted above, the light meter is aiming for middle gray, but it doesn't know what you're photographing. So if you're photographing a very bright scene (such as snow), you'll want to "overexpose" the scene and give it a bit more light, with the meter's needle going into the "+" (plus) side of the scale. (This will ensure the snow looks white rather than a dull gray.) For a dark scene, "underexpose" by having the light meter's needle going into the "–" (minus) side of the scale.

Many film shooters like to shoot with settings that give a slight overexposure. When shooting film, it's better to slightly overexpose than it is to underexpose, which can lead to muddy-looking photographs. Give it a try and see if you like the results.

Note: If your camera's built-in light meter is not working, or if your camera doesn't have one, try a light meter app on your smartphone (such as Pocket Light Meter) to help you dial in the correct exposure.

THE "SUNNY 16" RULE

A handy exposure guideline that photographers use is the Sunny 16 rule. It's pretty simple: On a sunny day, when your subject is in the sun, set your aperture to f/16, and you should be able to get a decent exposure by setting your shutter speed to 1/ISO. For example, if your film's ISO is 100, set your shutter speed to 1/100.

Note, though, that if your subject is in the shadows on a sunny day, you'll want to open up your exposure by a stop or two (going from f/16 to f/11 or even f/8) to make sure that your subject is properly exposed.

EXPOSURE CHART FOR SHOOTING FILM

It makes good sense to use your camera's light meter (or a light meter app) to help determine the correct exposure, but you can also use this handy exposure chart to check your settings and help confirm that you are on the right track.

CONDITIONS	SUNNY	LIGHT CLOUDS	CLOUDY	OVERCAST	SUNSET
APERTURE	SHUTTER SPEED AT ISO 100				
f/16	1/100	1/50	1/25	1/12	1/6
f/11	1/200	1/100	1/50	1/25	1/12
f/8	1/400	1/200	1/100	1/50	1/25
f/5.6	1/800	1/400	1/200	1/100	1/50
f/4	1/1600	1/800	1/400	1/200	1/100
f/2.8	1/3200	1/1600	1/800	1/400	1/200

04 BEYOND MANUAL MODE

If you've got a more modern film camera that has more advanced capabilities, you may have some of the following features, which can be very handy in helping you get the shot.

EXPOSURE/SHOOTING MODES

The exposure/shooting mode that you choose tells the camera how to help you create the exposure. There are three main exposure/shooting modes to choose from:

Program Auto: The camera determines the exposure by setting the shutter speed and the aperture. The photographer has little control over exposure.

Aperture Priority: *This is the most popular shooting mode, and the most commonly used for most situations.* The photographer sets the aperture, and the camera sets the shutter speed. Best when you want to control the depth of field to either have the subject pop off a blurred background (example: using f/2.8 for a shallow depth of field) or when you need to make sure that all the elements in the image are in focus (example: using f/22 for a deep depth of field).

Shutter Speed Priority: The photographer sets the shutter speed, and the camera picks the aperture. This is best used when you want to make sure that you are controlling how motion is conveyed in the photograph—that it is either frozen (with a fast shutter speed) or creatively blurred (with a slower shutter speed).

Note: Some cameras have additional modes (such as Scene modes or other Auto modes), but these three modes are the main exposure/shooting modes that all the other modes are based on.

METERING MODES

As noted earlier, in order to determine what the camera thinks is the right exposure, it uses a built-in light meter to analyze and measure the light in the scene. This measuring process is called metering, and the metering modes in your camera measure light in different ways. The camera uses this information to determine what it thinks are the proper exposure settings for your photo. These are the three main metering modes:

Evaluative/Matrix: The camera examines the whole scene to determine the exposure. This is the best setting for most photography and is the recommended metering mode for most situations.

Spot: The camera looks at just a small spart of the scene and ignores the rest. This is best when you have large areas around your subject that are either very dark or very bright (such as an actor on a stage), and you do not want the camera to factor these areas into the exposure.

Center-Weighted: The camera analyzes and gives priority to the central, main part of the scene in order to measure the light, and it ignores the outer edges of the scene.

EXPOSURE COMPENSATION

When you are shooting in Program Auto, Aperture Priority, or Shutter Speed Priority mode, the camera is determining at least one of the exposure settings, and sometimes the overall exposure will not be the result you want—the image will be too dark or too bright. The exposure compensation feature allows you to adjust the exposure settings to make the photo lighter ("+" [plus] compensation) or darker ("–" [minus] compensation).

This is a very powerful feature. Most photographers use exposure compensation in coordination with shooting in Aperture Priority or Shutter Speed Priority mode. Most cameras allow exposure compensation settings of up to three or more stops, in 1/3-stop or one-stop increments.

Note: When shooting in Manual mode with a camera that has these kinds of features, exposure compensation is unavailable—to make the overall exposure brighter or darker, you simply change the aperture or shutter speed yourself.

FOCUS AREA AND FOCUS MODES

The focus area refers to what portion of the scene you tell the camera to use to determine focus. Cameras use focus points, either individually or grouped in varying sizes, to allow you to pick the critical area in the image to focus on.

The focus mode is the method that the camera uses to achieve focus. The main focus modes are:

Single Shot Auto Focus: *The most commonly used mode for most situations.* The camera focuses until the focus is achieved, then the focus is locked and doesn't change again until you either take the photo or remove pressure from the shutter release button. Best used for stationary subjects.

Continuous Auto Focus: The camera keeps focusing right up to the point when the photo is taken. Best used for moving subjects. (This mode is also sometimes called "Servo" mode.)

Manual Focus: You rotate the lens barrel's focus ring to focus the lens. Best used when the autofocus modes are not focusing on the exact area you want them to—or, of course, if your camera doesn't have autofocus capability.

RELEASE/DRIVE MODES

The release/drive mode determines how the camera captures photographs when you press the shutter release button:

Single Release: *The most commonly used method for most situations.* The camera takes a single image every time the shutter release button is pressed all the way down.

Continuous Release: The camera keeps taking photos as long as the shutter button is pressed all the way down (and there is film left to shoot!).

Self-Timer: The camera takes a photo after a predetermined amount of time passes after the shutter release is pressed all the way down. Many cameras offer a 2-second and 10-second self-timer.

Bulb: The shutter will stay open as long as the shutter release is pressed down. On some cameras, you can press the shutter release once to start the exposure and a second time to end it. You can also often control the shutter release with a cable release.

05 LENSES AND FOCAL LENGTH

In addition to your choices of aperture and/or shutter speed, the other factor that has a massive influence on the look of your photo is your choice of lens—more specifically, your choice of focal length.

FOCAL LENGTHS

The focal length of a lens is described in millimeters (mm) and measures the distance from the optical center of the lens to the camera's film plane. The focal length determines the angle of view of the lens. The smaller the number, the wider the angle of view.

Ultra Wide Angle: Lenses with a focal length of 24mm or less

Wide Angle: Lenses with a focal length of 24mm to 35mm

Standard: Lenses with a focal length of 35mm to 70mm

Telephoto: Lenses with a focal length between 70mm and 300mm

Super Telephoto: Lenses with a focal length of more than 300mm

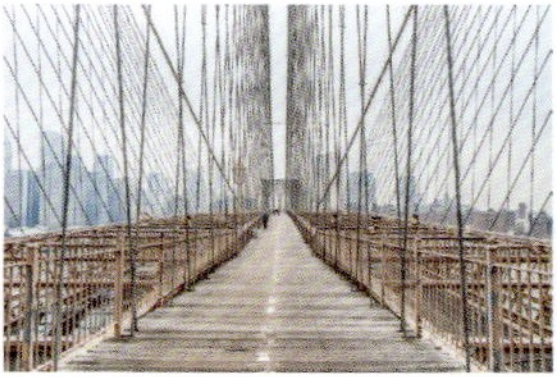

24mm

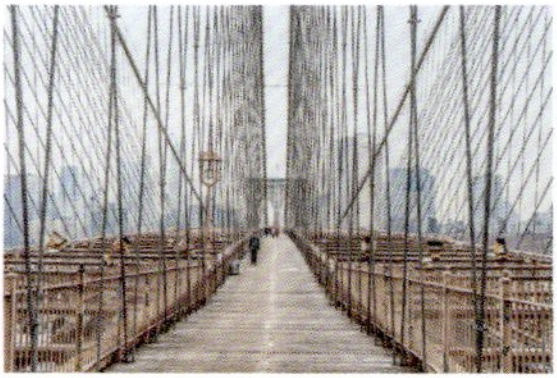

40mm

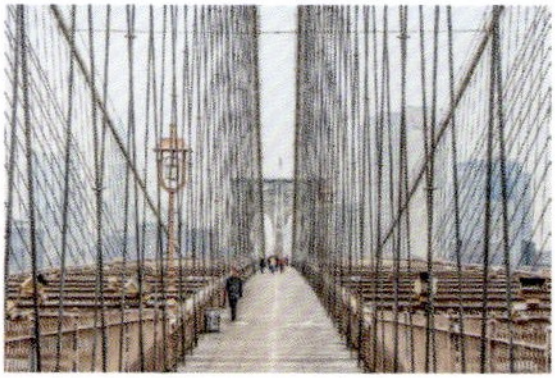

75mm

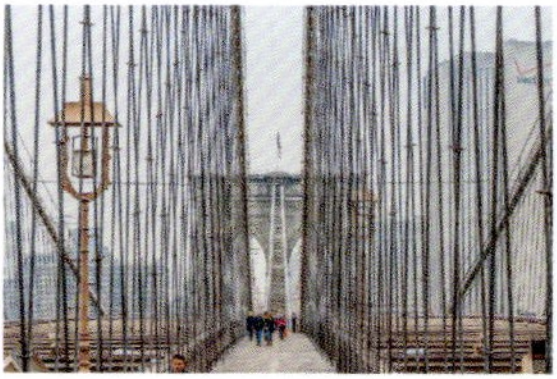

120mm

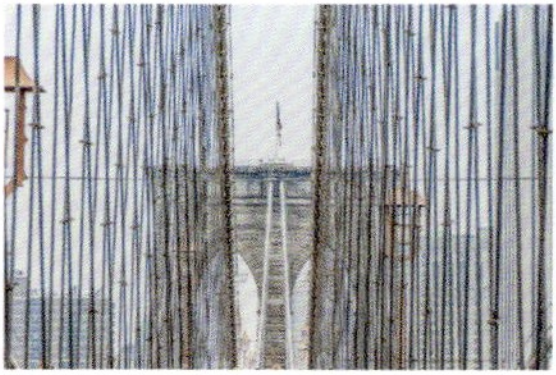

200mm

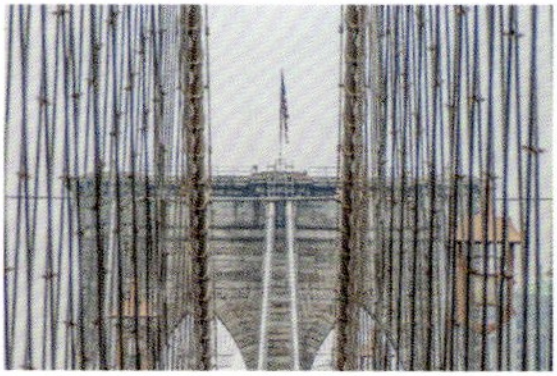

300mm

Prime lenses have a single, nonadjustable focal length (such as a 50mm lens) while **zoom lenses** cover a range of focal lengths (such as a 70–200mm lens).

Your choice of lens depends on the subject matter and how you want to capture it. This is not a hard and fast rule by any means, but landscape photography is often captured with ultra wide angle and wide angle lenses, while portraits are often captured with standard and telephoto lenses. Your choice of focal length can have a dramatic effect on how the subject is rendered in a photo (see the next section).

LENS COMPRESSION AND DISTORTION

Just as the tools of exposure have both a technical purpose and creative effect, the focal length behaves similarly. Your choice of lens and focal length can greatly impact not just how the subject looks, but how the subject is shown in relationship to the background and foreground.

A wide angle lens includes more of the scene, and it also "spreads out" the elements in the scene to make them look farther apart. It also has the effect of distorting subjects that are very close to the camera. Wide angle lenses are typically good for landscape photography but are often not a great choice for portrait photography.

A telephoto lens, on the other hand, compresses the scene and makes it seem like the background is much closer to the subject. This quality of "compression" is also considered very flattering for portrait photography.

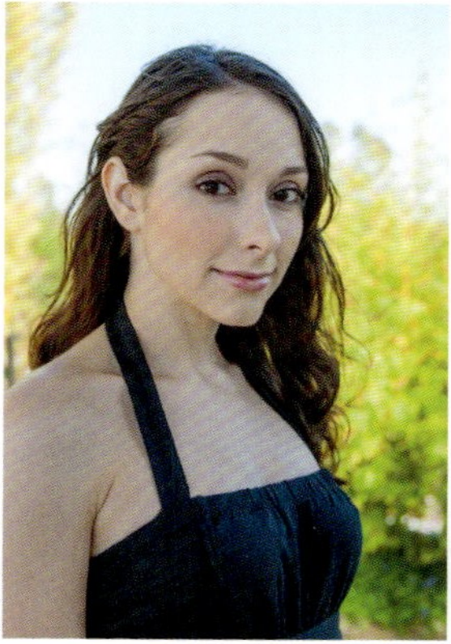

24mm (wide angle)

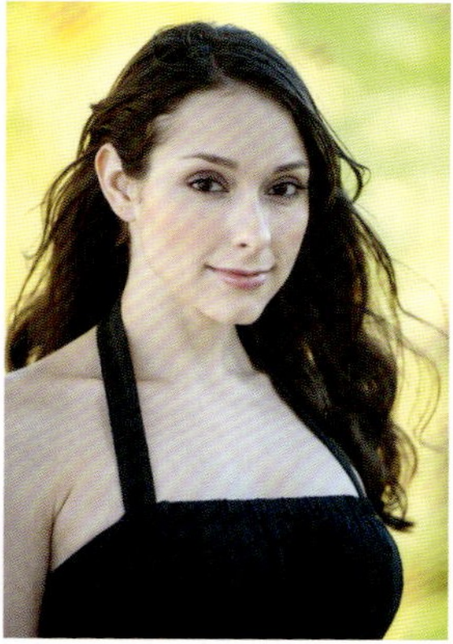

200mm (telephoto)

You can use longer focal lengths (85mm or more) to isolate your subject from their surroundings and, especially when combined with a shallow depth of field (via a large aperture such as f/2.8), the background will blur and your subject will stand out.

FOCAL LENGTH, CAMERA SHAKE, AND SHUTTER SPEED

The longer the focal length, the faster the shutter speed should be to avoid camera shake that can blur your image, making it appear soft or out of focus. The guideline to use is that your shutter speed should be equal to 1/focal length. For example, using a 200mm lens requires a minimum shutter speed of 1/200".

IMAGE STABILIZATION/VIBRATION REDUCTION

Your lens may have the option to turn on an image stabilization feature. Turn this feature on when hand-holding your camera to help ensure a sharp image, especially when shooting at slower shutter speeds (such as 1/30" or slower).

Note: When shooting on a tripod, turn off the image stabilization feature, as it may actually cause motion blur as the feature "seeks" movement to stabilize.

06 ADVANCED SHOOTING TECHNIQUES

BACK BUTTON FOCUS

On cameras that have autofocus capabilities, the default is to have the camera begin focusing when the shutter release button is pressed halfway down. This ties the focusing operation to taking the picture. But on many cameras, you can separate these functions by assigning focus operation to a different button—such as one of the back buttons on the camera. This allows you to start and stop focusing separately from taking the photo. Back button focus is often used by sports photographers who need to stop and start focusing as players and officials run through their frame, but many photographers prefer this setup for all of their photography.

FOCUS AND COMPOSITION

If you're using a manual-only camera, the only way to achieve focus is manually: to turn the focus barrel on your lens until your subject is in sharp focus.

But if you're using a camera with autofocus features, there are two main methods you can use to achieve sharp focus when using autofocus with one single focus point:

Focus and recompose: *The most common method.* When shooting most stationary subjects with Single Shot autofocus, you can place the single focus point over the subject, achieve focus (by either pressing and holding the shutter button half-way down or using the back button focus method), and then recompose your image and take the shot.

Move the focus point: Many cameras have a large number of focus points that cover the majority of the frame, which allows you to compose the scene first, then move the focus point so it is directly over the most critical area in the image (such as the eye of a portrait subject), and then take the shot.

BRACKETING EXPOSURES

Bracketing is a technique where you take a series of images with a set exposure difference (such as one or two stops) between each photo. Usually a bracketed sequence will be three photos.

The reason you might want to bracket your exposures is, for example, if you're in a tricky lighting situation or witnessing a rare event (or both) and you want to make sure you get a proper exposure. In this case, you would take one "normal" exposure based on your light meter, then take one shot underexposed by a stop, and finally, take one more shot overexposed by a stop.

Yes, you're using three frames to capture one scene/moment, but you're increasing the chances that you'll have a shot that you're happy with later.

PUSHING AND PULLING FILM

The terms "pushing" and "pulling" film refer to a technique where you shoot with an ISO setting on your camera's ISO dial that is different from the ISO rating of your film. "Pushing" means that you are purposely underexposing your film by setting your camera to a higher ISO than the film. "Pulling" is the opposite: purposely overexposing your film by setting your camera to a lower ISO than the film. (Note: pushing film is a much more commonly used technique than pulling film.) There are two main reasons to push or pull your film:

The practical reason is that you are shooting in lighting conditions that are not ideal for the ISO of the film you have. For example, you have ISO 200 film but are in a dark indoor setting. You could choose to "push your film two stops" by setting your camera's ISO to 800 (which is two stops more than 200: 200 > 400 > 800).

The aesthetic reason is that pushing and pulling film gives you a different look. Pulling film reduces contrast and can create a faded look. Pushing film increases contrast and can create a bit more drama in the images.

If you choose to push or pull your film, it is *absolutely crucial* that you indicate to the film lab developing the film that you have pushed or pulled the film, and by how much (one stop, two stops, etc.). The lab will adjust their developing process accordingly, which will compensate for the (intentional) under- or overexposure of the film that you created when pushing or pulling the film.

07 COMPOSITION TIPS AND SHOOTING SCENARIOS

RULE OF THIRDS

Divide the scene with two equally spaced vertical lines and two equally spaced horizontal lines, then place the subject where the lines intersect. For landscape photography, try placing the horizon line at the top or bottom third of the frame (one of the "rule of thirds" horizontal lines). For portrait photography, try aligning the eyes with the top third of the frame.

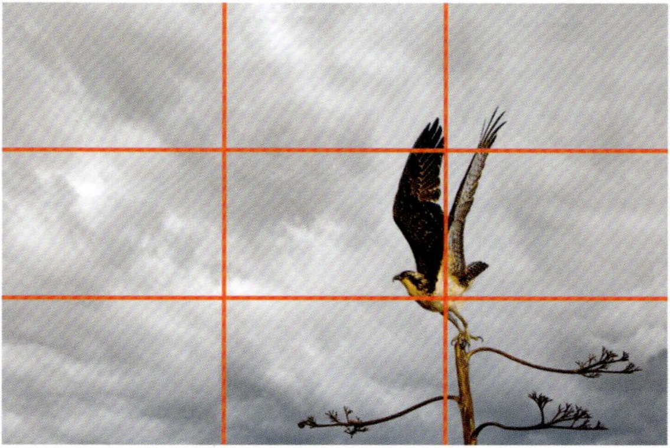

Note: Of course, all rules are meant to be broken! Sometimes a great photograph will show the subject in the middle of the frame (often called "bull's eye" framing). The rule of thirds is not so much a "rule" as a guide. Just remember: you decide where the subject goes in your frame.

FILL THE FRAME

Get in close and make the subject a significant part of the whole frame.

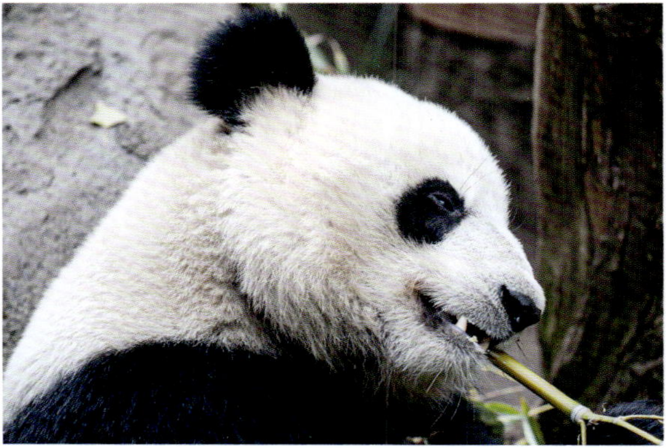

NEGATIVE SPACE

While you should "fill the frame" (see previous page) so it's clear what your subject is, you can also balance that by leaving some room for the subject to "breathe" in your photo. A practical example: If your subject is moving or looking in a certain direction, leave space in front of them in your composition.

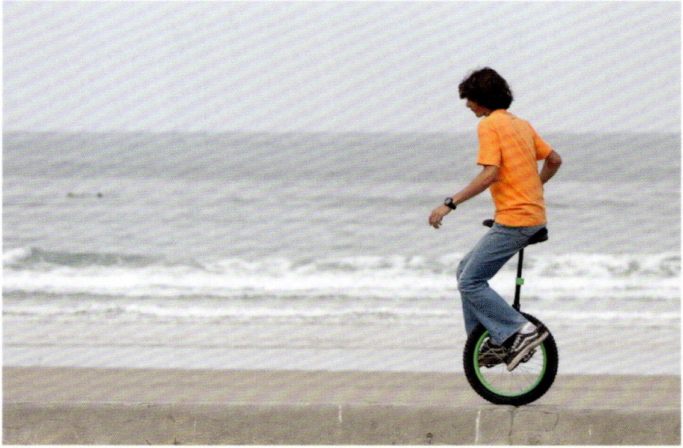

LEADING LINES

Look for lines that naturally occur in the scene, and then use them to direct the viewer's eye to the subject. Leading lines can be actual lines (such as a road) or an implied line (such as a row of trees).

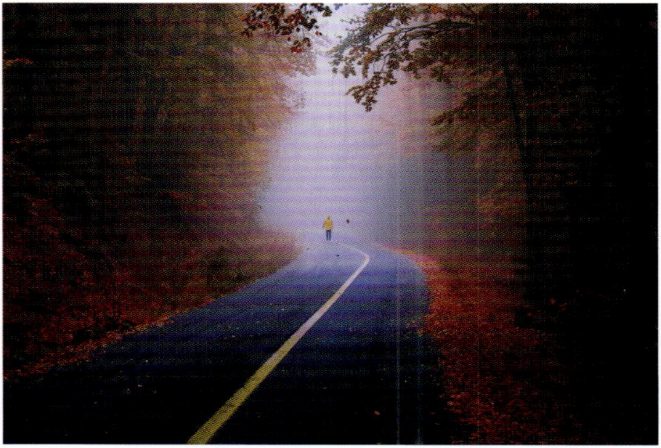

PATTERNS AND REPETITION

Patterns draw the eye in a photograph, and repetition of the item, shape, or color can create a pleasing symmetry. You can also deliberately interrupt that pattern to create even more impact.

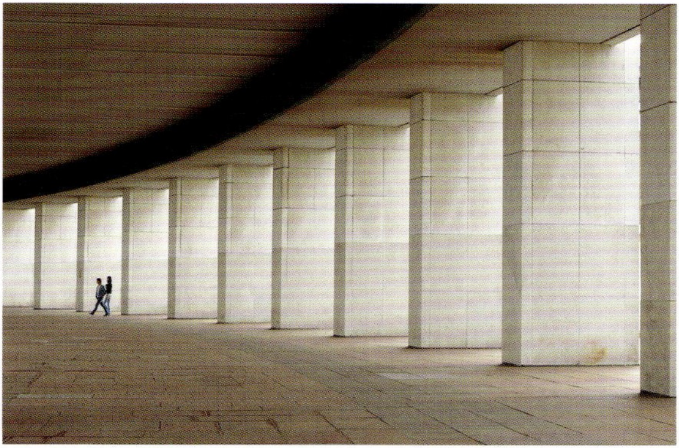

FRAME WITHIN A FRAME

Use a visual element in your scene, such as a window, door, or archway to frame your subject. Make sure that the framing device is clear of distractions and doesn't have any elements that could lead the eye out of the frame.

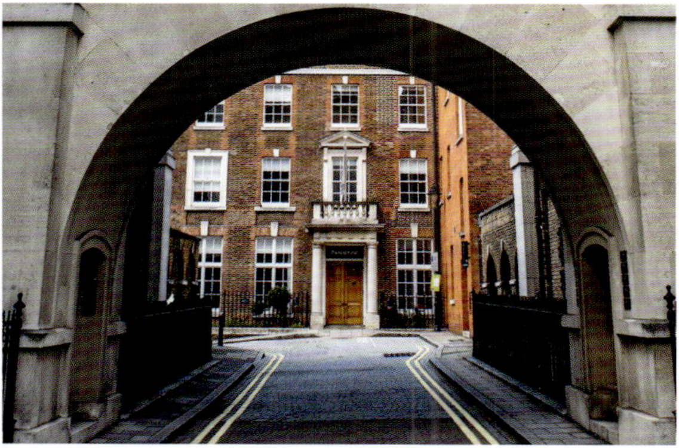

POINT OF VIEW

The placement of the camera in relation to the subject can drastically change the way the photo is viewed. Go low or high to change the relationship of the subject to the background. Try different shooting positions! Don't just shoot everything at your own eye level.

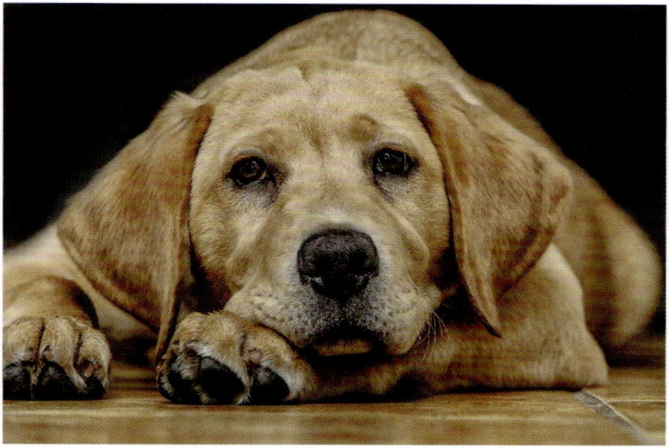

COLOR

Use color to grab the viewer's attention. You can also look for situations with complementary colors—such as yellow and blue, or red and green. Ask yourself if the color itself is the subject of the image. For example, in the photo below, would the blue wall and yellow window box have the same impact if they were not this colorful?

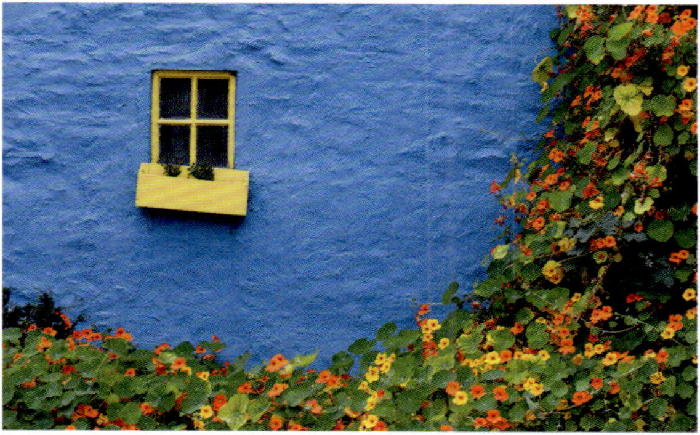

BLACK AND WHITE

When your subject matter is heavily textured or your scene contains strong graphical elements, try black and white for a powerful impression. Sometimes a photo can become stronger by showing it in simple, monochromatic black and white.

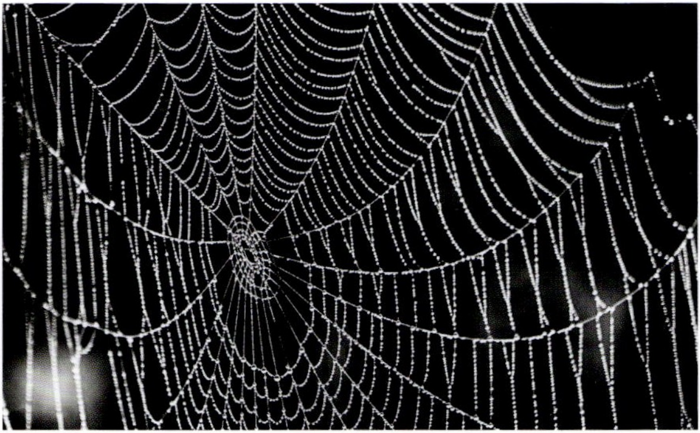

WATCH THE BACKGROUND

Avoid items in the background that could detract from or interact negatively with the subject. The classic example is a distracting element in the background (such as a tree limb) emerging from a portrait subject's head.

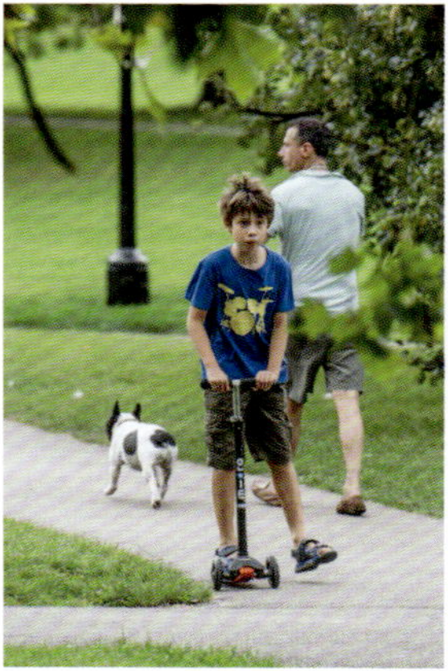

Bad background

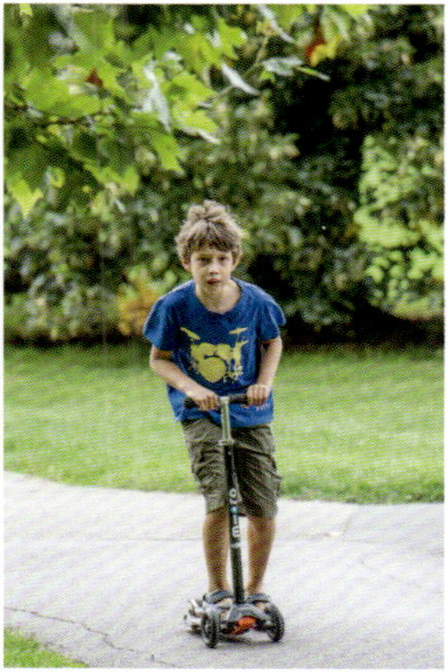

Clean background

SIMPLIFY

The strongest compositions are often simple. Look for different ways to compose your image using all the tools at your disposal, including your point of view, choice of focal length, depth of field, and shutter speed.

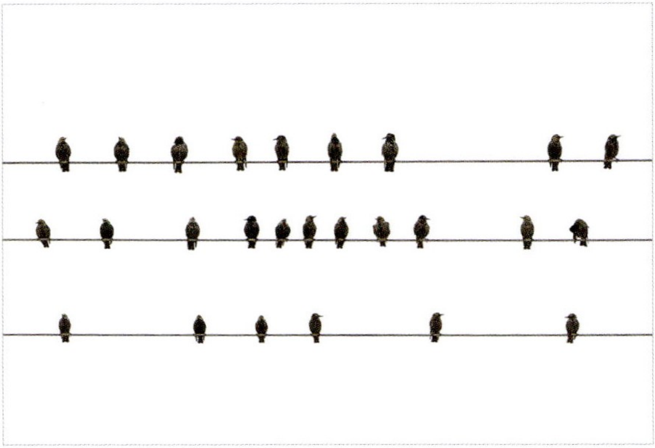

FIND GREAT LIGHT

This may sound obvious, but great light makes a big difference in your photos. Pay attention to the light. When the light is wonderful, you have automatically improved your chances of getting a great shot.

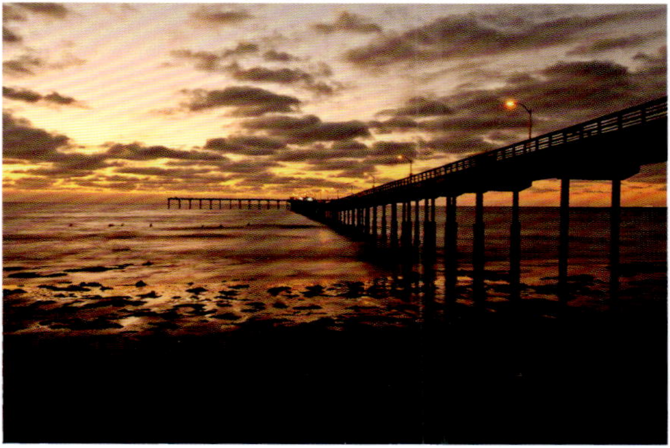

SHOOTING SCENARIO

PORTRAIT

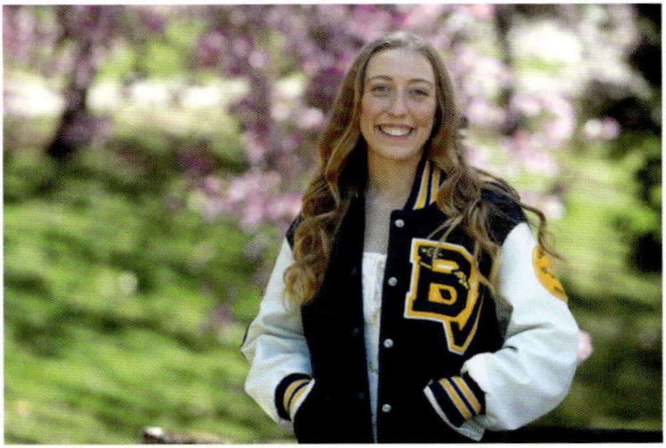

KEY PRINCIPLES

- The key to a portrait like this is shallow depth of field. For manual-only shooters, **prioritize using a low aperture such as f/2.8 or f/4**. With a more modern camera, try shooting in **APERTURE PRIORITY** mode.
- Remember to **focus on the eyes**.
- Remember to **use a focal length of 50mm or greater** so that you don't distort your subject's face.

SHOOTING SCENARIO

GROUP PORTRAIT

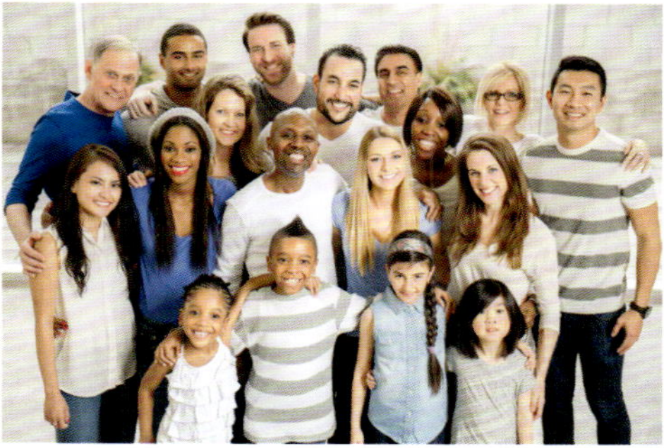

KEY PRINCIPLES

- In order to get everyone in focus, you need a deep depth of field. So, **shoot with an aperture set between f/8–f/16**.
- **Focus on the person in the middle of the group**.
- Use **EVALUATIVE/MATRIX** metering (if your camera has this feature) to account for the light in the entire scene.
- **Arrange the group so they can all see you** (and you can see them).

SHOOTING SCENARIO

LANDSCAPE

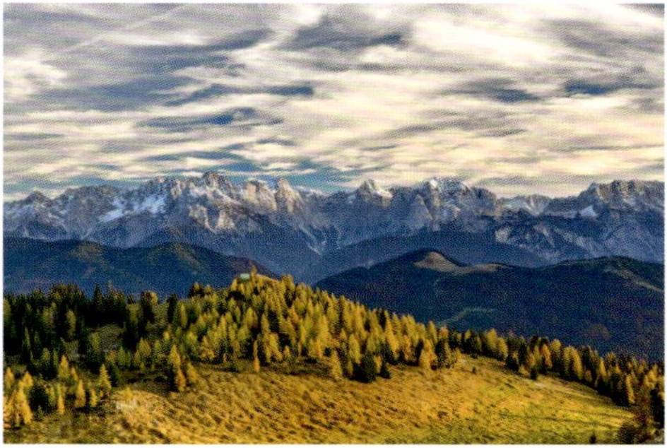

KEY PRINCIPLES

- **Shoot with a deep depth of field** by using an aperture such as f/16.
- **Use a tripod** to eliminate camera movement. Whenever your camera is on a tripod, also make sure that the lens **IMAGE STABILIZATION/VIBRATION REDUCTION is turned OFF** (if your camera has this feature).
- Use **EVALUATIVE/MATRIX** metering mode and **SINGLE SHOT AUTO FOCUS** mode (if your camera has these features).

- Consider **BRACKETING** your exposures to make sure you get a great shot.
- Consider a **low ISO film like Velvia 50** for rich, saturated colors.

SHOOTING SCENARIO
FREEZE ACTION

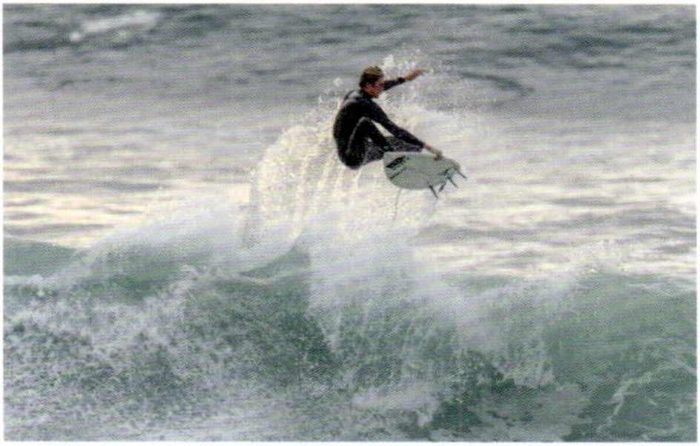

KEY PRINCIPLES

- Use a shutter speed that will freeze the action. For manual-only shooters, **prioritize using a fast shutter speed**; with a more modern camera, use **SHUTTER SPEED PRIORITY** mode. The appropriate shutter speed depends on your subject and its movement, but could be anywhere between **1/500"–1/2000"**.

- With such fast shutter speeds, it will be helpful to **use a higher-ISO film, such as ISO 400, 800, or 1600**.
- Use **CONTINUOUS AUTO FOCUS** mode (if your camera has this feature) so that the camera keeps focusing as the subject moves.

SHOOTING SCENARIO
SHOWING MOTION—PANNING

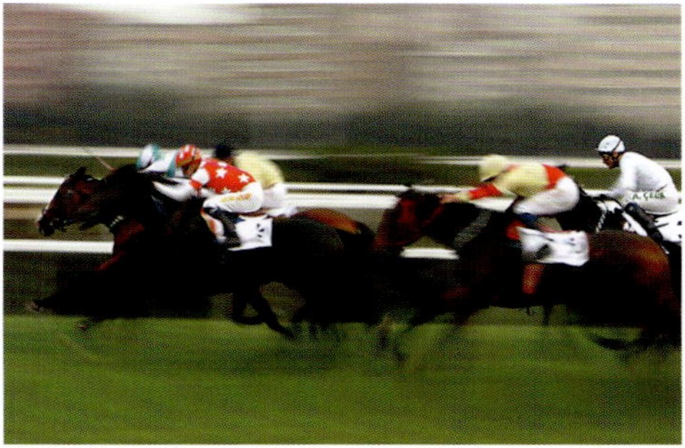

KEY PRINCIPLES

- **Prioritize the shutter speed** and use a slow-enough shutter speed to allow for the subject to move during the exposure. The proper shutter speed depends on the situation, but **1/30"** is a good starting point.

- **Follow the subject** across the frame as you shoot.
- Use **CONTINUOUS AUTO FOCUS** mode (if your camera has this feature), and **keep the focus point on the subject** as the subject and camera both move.

SHOOTING SCENARIO
LOW-LIGHT SITUATIONS

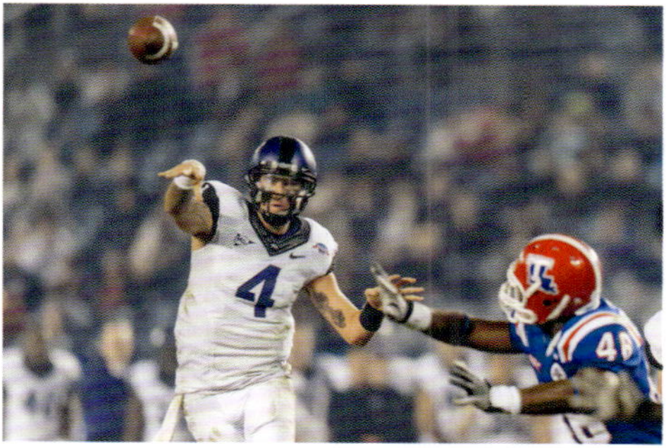

KEY PRINCIPLES

- Use a wide aperture such as f/2.8 or f/4. With a more modern camera, try shooting in **APERTURE PRIORITY** mode.
- Use **SPOT** metering (if your camera has this feature) and **meter on the subject's face**.

- Use **CONTINUOUS AUTO FOCUS** and a **single autofocus point** (if your camera has these features).
- Use an **ISO 1600 or 3200** film to help ensure you'll have a fast enough shutter speed to freeze the action.

SHOOTING SCENARIO
LONG EXPOSURE

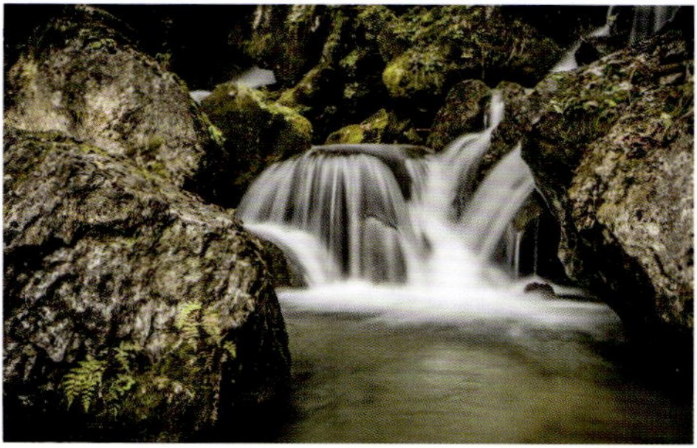

KEY PRINCIPLES

- Use your camera's **BULB** setting to allow for long exposures.
- **Use a tripod** to keep the camera stable. **Turn off any IMAGE STABILIZATION/VIBRATION REDUCTION** feature on your lens (if applicable).

- Use the **SINGLE SHOT AUTO FOCUS** mode (if applicable) or **switch to manual focus** if the camera is having a hard time locking on focus.
- **Use a low-rated ISO film** (such as ISO 50, 100, or 200) to help allow for a long exposure.
- Consider using a **cable release** to fire the camera without touching (and thus shaking) it.

SHOOTING SCENARIO
MACRO/CLOSE-UP

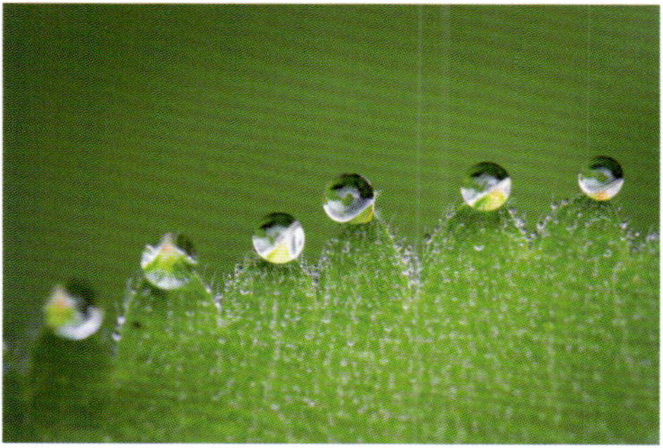

KEY PRINCIPLES

- **Shoot with a small aperture** to ensure you achieve enough depth of field. When the camera is so close to the subject, the depth of field can be extremely shallow, so a small aperture helps here (this image was shot at f/13). With a more modern camera, try shooting in **APERTURE PRIORITY** mode.

- Use **EVALUATIVE/MATRIX** metering (if your camera has this feature) to analyze the light in the entire frame.
- **Use a tripod** to keep the camera steady. **Turn off any IMAGE STABILIZATION/VIBRATION REDUCTION** feature (if applicable) on your lens.
- Try **manual focus** to confirm that your focus is tack-sharp.
- Try using a dedicated **macro lens or close-up filters** to make sure you can achieve sharp focus when you are so close to the subject.